A Jewish Holiday A·B·C

MALKA DRUCKER · RITA POCOCK

Gulliver Books

Harcourt Brace Jovanovich, Publishers

San Diego　　New York　　London

Text copyright © 1992 by Malka Drucker
Illustrations copyright © 1992 by Rita Pocock

Requests for permission to make copies of any part of
the work should be mailed to: Permissions Department,
Harcourt Brace Jovanovich, Publishers, 8th Floor, Orlando, Florida 32887.

Library of Congress Cataloging-in-Publication Data
Drucker, Malka.
A Jewish holiday ABC/by Malka Drucker;
illustrated by Rita Pocock. — 1st ed.
p.   cm.
"Gulliver books."
Summary: An alphabet book introducing Jewish holidays and their customs.
ISBN 0-15-200482-3
1. Fasts and feasts — Judaism — Juvenile literature.
[1. Fasts and feasts — Judaism. 2. Alphabet.]
I. Pocock, Rita, ill. II. Title.
BM690.D78   1992
296.4'3 — dc20
[E]   90-36791

7903

First edition   A B C D E

For Barbara Karlin,
whose eloquence, laughter, and friendship
have enriched my life.
—M. D.

For Mom and B. D.
—R. P.

The illustrations in this book were done in collage with colored pencil.
The display type and text type were set in Goudy Old Style
by Thompson Type, San Diego, California.
Color separations were made by Bright Arts, Ltd., Singapore.
Printed and bound by Tien Wah Press, Singapore
Production supervision by Warren Wallerstein and Ginger Boyer
Designed by Camilla Filancia

A Near the end of the Passover seder, Rachel finds the **afikomen** hidden under the tablecloth.

B Raffy brings a **bow** and arrows and watches the bonfire at the Lag B'omer picnic.

C As the sun goes down, Minnie and her mother sing the prayer that blesses the Shabbat **candles**.

D On the first night of Chanukah, Raffy, Morris, and Minnie sing and spin the **dreidel**. The winner gets a pile of nuts.

E Each time Minnie eats lunch in the sukkah, she sniffs the sweet **etrog** and shakes the tall lulav.

F On Simhat Torah, Morris and Raffy dance around the synagogue holding the Torah and waving blue and white **flags**.

G On Purim, Raffy shakes and grinds his **grogger** each time the Megillah reader shouts "Haman!"

H

Minnie's hands are sticky on Rosh Hashanah from eating apples dipped in **honey** for a sweet new year.

I On Yom Ha'Atzma'ut, **Israel's** birthday, Raffy, Morris, Minnie, and their cousin, Maxie, eat ice cream and watch fireworks.

J Every Yom Kippur, Morris shivers when he reads the story of **Jonah** being swallowed by a whale.

K

Rachel holds the cup high when she sings the **Kiddush** on Shabbat.

L For the eight days of Chanukah, Maxie loves to eat **latkes** dripping with applesauce.

M Minnie tries to share her **matzah** with Morris at the Passover seder, but the flat, bumpy bread breaks into many pieces.

N After **Neilah**, the last service of Yom Kippur, Morris tells Minnie it's time to eat.

O As Safte fries the latkes in **oil**, she tells the grandchildren that we eat latkes at Chanukah because of the miracle of the oil.

P On Passover, Raffy sings the **prayers** he learned in Hebrew School to the family sitting around the table.

Q "Quick, the parade is beginning! Put on your **Queen Esther** costume for Purim!" Rachel shouts to Minnie.

R On Rosh Hashanah, Raffy races to the synagogue to hear the **rabbi** blow the shofar.

S On Saturday morning, Minnie says, "Shabbat **shalom**" to everyone she sees.

The **Torah** tells the story of the Jewish people. On Shavuot, Rachel takes tulips to the synagogue to say thanks for the Torah.

U

Rosh Hashanah is the birthday of the **universe**.
Mother sings "Happy Birthday to You."

V In the fall, Morris and Raffy fill the sukkah with fruits and **vegetables**.

W

Rachel and Raffy leave the table at the Passover seder to **wash** their hands together.

X The Chanukah candles are almost melted when Morris opens his biggest box and finds a **xylophone** inside.

Y

On Yom Kippur, Morris and Raffy wear white **yarmulkes**. Rachel and Minnie wear them, too.

Z Zayde leads the whole family while they sing Shabbat **zemirot**.

About the Holidays

Each Jewish holiday has its own rituals and purpose, but they all begin at sundown with the lighting of candles and the giving of tzedakah, money to those in need. The Torah says: "You shall surely open your hand to your poor and needy kin" (*Deuteronomy* 15:11). Rabbis have interpreted this to mean that although one shouldn't wait for a holiday to help someone else, the holidays do provide an additional chance to ease suffering.

SHABBAT   (shah-BAHT)

Shabbat, the day of rest, is celebrated each Saturday, the seventh day of the week. Except for Yom Kippur, no holiday is more important. Shabbat follows the pattern of Creation, when God worked for six days to make the world and rested on the seventh. The weekly festival, which celebrates the creation of the world and the creativity of the human spirit, also includes animals and plants in the commandment to rest. Shabbat begins Friday night at sundown with the lighting and blessing of at least two candles. When three stars appear in the sky on Saturday night, the holiday, also called "The Day of Delight," is over.

ROSH HASHANAH   ([ROW]SH hah-shah-NAH)

Rosh Hashanah marks the start of the Jewish year and usually falls in late September or early October. It celebrates the beginning of the world and the creation of human beings. While most Jewish holidays celebrate historical events, Rosh Hashanah focuses on the individual. It is a joyful but solemn festival, the time when a person faces the mistakes of the past year and asks forgiveness of anyone he or she has harmed. Blowing the shofar during the prayers in the synagogue is supposed to awaken the spirit to self-examination. Everyone hopes that the year will be sweet as apples and honey, which is why they are part of the festive meal.

YOM KIPPUR   (YOME key-POOR)

Yom Kippur means "Day of Cleansing." On Kol Nidre, the night before the day of Yom Kippur, everyone fills the synagogue to participate in the most important holiday of the calendar, even those Jews who may only attend services once a year. Jews may not eat, drink, work, or go to school on Yom Kippur. They spend most of the day in the synagogue reading from the Torah and reciting special prayers that offer people the courage to make a fresh start. Fasting isn't intended as a punishment but rather as a reminder of how dependent people are upon God and upon one another for food. The fast is also a way to remember the suffering of the poor and hungry.

Neilah is the last service of Yom Kippur and ends at sundown when everyone goes home, eager to break the fast with a family meal. Immediately after the dinner, the custom is to hammer in the first nail of the sukkah as a way to shift from reflection to deed.

SUKKOT   (soo-COAT)

Sukkot, which falls five days after Yom Kippur, celebrates the fall harvest and the forty years that the Jewish people wandered in the wilderness. Sukkot means "booths," the temporary shelters the Jews lived in during their journey to the promised land. The most joyful holiday of the Jewish calendar, it is celebrated by building and decorating a little hut, called a sukkah, with fruits and vegetables. Some people actually live in the sukkah for the week-long holiday. Others simply eat meals in it and invite friends and family to share in the celebration. During Sukkot, one prays with a lulav and an etrog, shaking them in all directions to acknowledge God's sovereignty over the natural world.

SIMHAT TORAH   (sim-[k]HOT toe-RAH)

Simhat Torah means "Rejoicing of the Torah." This holiday, which is the last day of Sukkot, celebrates the annual completion of Torah readings. Divided into weekly portions, the Torah is read and discussed each Shabbat all year round. On Simhat Torah, both the last and first portions are read. The congregation, including the children, gathers for a service where all the Torahs are carried in a march around the synagogue and small children wave Israeli flags with an apple speared on top.

CHANUKAH   ([k]HAH-noo-kuh)

Chanukah is an eight-day celebration that usually falls in December. This "Feast of Dedication" is a holiday of opposites. On the one hand, the holiday is a delight — eight days of songs, games, candlelight, gifts, and special foods. On the other hand, the holiday recalls the violent Chanukah story about the first great war for religious freedom. The war not only saved the Jewish people from annihilation but also showed how a small group of people triumphed over impossible odds in their struggle for the right to practice their beliefs. Each night of the holiday is marked by lighting a small candle (the candles are lit from right to left) in a nine-branched candelabra called a menorah. This is a reminder that when the Maccabees, the victorious Jewish warriors, returned to the Temple after they had driven out Antiochus the dictator, they called for an eight-day celebration. But they discovered that they had only enough oil to light the Eternal Lamp for one day. Miraculously, the oil lasted for eight days. Chanukah is about miracles: the miracle of the oil and of the Maccabean victory. Most of all, it's about the miracle of the inner spirit which gives courage and strength amidst overwhelming struggles.

PURIM   (poo-REAM)

Purim is a holiday for laughter, costumes, puppet shows, and giving delicious treats to friends, including hamentaschen — triangular cookies filled with poppy seed or jam. On Purim a reader chants the Megillah, the story of how, in Persia, Haman tried to kill the Jews and how Queen Esther and her uncle Mordechai defeated him. Each time Haman's name is said, everyone shakes noisemakers called groggers to drown it out. Tradition has it that in the world to come, only Purim will be celebrated, because the mitzvah for Purim is laughter, and a human being will always need laughter to live. Just as there was a great celebration following Haman's end, so Jews gather in early spring to remember the event by reading the Megillah and to celebrate Jewish survival then and now.

PASSOVER (PASS-oh-ver)

Passover is a week-long festival that marks the spring season and the birth of the Jewish people. It is the oldest Jewish holiday. The highlight of the festival is the seder, a ritual evening meal recalling the exodus of the Israelites from Egypt. The first half of the seder focuses on the historic slavery of the Jews. The second half centers on freedom and the hope of a better world to come. Seder foods, arranged on a large seder plate, are unusual as well as tasty. The plate contains parsley, to symbolize spring; charoset, a mixture of apples, walnuts, wine, and honey, to represent the mortar the enslaved Israelites used when constructing buildings for the Pharaoh; horseradish, a bitter herb to recall the bitterness of slavery; and a shankbone to symbolize the animal sacrifice the Israelites made to God before departing from Egypt. Parsley is dipped into salt water to remember the tears of suffering. Matzah, unleavened crackerlike bread, is eaten as a reminder that the Israelites' escape was so rushed there was no time to let the bread dough rise.

YOM HA'ATZMA'UT (YOME hah-ahtz-mah-OOT)

Yom Ha'Atzma'ut, Israeli Independence Day, is celebrated May 14, the day in 1948 that Israel was declared a state by the United Nations. The eve of the holiday is celebrated with fireworks, dancing in the streets, parties, and outdoor concerts. On the day itself, Israelis go on picnics and to sports events. There are also special services in the synagogue, where most Jews outside Israel celebrate the day that gave the Jewish people, after two thousand years, a country where they knew they would always belong and be welcome.

LAG B'OMER (lahg bah-OWE-mare)

Lag B'omer is one holiday in the forty-nine-day period between Passover and Shavuot, during which farmers brought an omer of barley to the Temple each day as a thanksgiving offering to God. This period between Passover and Shavuot is called "counting the omer" and is a time of mourning because it is when 12,000 of Rabbi Akiba's followers were killed by the Romans. Lag B'omer is a day of respite from the mourning, the only day of the forty-nine on which a wedding can be held, and the only day when a haircut is allowed. The holiday has special meaning for students, because it commemorates the day on which a plague that had killed thousands of Akiba's students suddenly stopped. Simeon Bar Yohai, a great teacher, lived at the same time as Akiba, and he escaped the Romans by hiding in a cave for thirteen years, living on water from a spring, and eating the fruit from a nearby carob tree. On Lag B'omer, his students came to visit him. To fool the Romans, they dressed as hunters and carried bows and arrows. Today the holiday is celebrated with picnics, bonfires, and bows and arrows.

SHAVUOT (shah-voo-OAT)

Shavuot falls at the end of the counting of the omer. It celebrates the moment when God gave Moses the Torah, including the Ten Commandments. The Torah, which includes the Five Books of Moses, is the holiest book of the Jewish people. Some people believe it contains everything there is to know in the world. On Shavuot there is a special service in the synagogue, which is filled with flowers to mark the late spring and to remember the ancient practice of bringing first fruits to the Temple in Jerusalem. Since the Torah, which gives nourishment to the spirit, is often likened to milk and honey, dairy foods such as blintzes and cheesecake are traditionally eaten on Shavuot.

Glossary

afikomen (ah-fi-KOE-men)   A half of a piece of matzah that is hidden during the seder and that must be found before the seder can end.

dreidel (DRAY-del)   A spinning top with four sides that is part of a game played during Chanukah.

etrog (et-[ROW]G)   A sweet-smelling citrus fruit grown in Israel that is one of the plants carried on Sukkot.

grogger (GRAH-ger)   Noisemakers at Purim. When the Megillah, the Book of Esther, is read in the synagogue, everyone makes a racket by shaking their noisemakers to drown out the sound every time they hear the name of the villain, Haman.

Haman (hah-MANN)   The villain of the Purim story. He tried to have all the Jews killed, but Queen Esther prevailed on her husband, King Ahasuerus, to save the Jews, and Haman ended up being hanged.

Jonah (JOE-nah)   Jonah's story is read from the Torah on Yom Kippur afternoon. When he tried to escape from God, Jonah fled to a ship where he was thrown overboard and swallowed by a whale. In desperation, Jonah prayed to God and was saved. In this way, Jonah learned there was no escaping God, just as there is no escaping one's conscience.

kiddush (key-DOOSH)   The blessing to welcome Shabbat and other holidays. It is usually said with wine.

latkes (LAHT-kus)   Potato pancakes fried in oil at Chanukah.

lulav (loo-LAWV)   A date palm. One of the plants carried on Sukkot.

matzah (MAHT-za)   A flat, lumpy cracker; unleavened bread. It is eaten at Passover because the Israelites escaped Egypt before their bread dough had time to rise.

mitzvah (MITZ-vah)   A commandment or good deed.

rabbi (RAB-bye)   Literally, "my teacher." Usually means Jewish spiritual leader.

safte (SAHF-tah)   Grandmother in Hebrew.

seder (SAY-der)   The most important meal of Passover, the seder is a dinner with talking, singing, praying, storytelling, and special foods.

shalom (shah-LOME)   Peace. Also a Hebrew greeting or farewell.

shofar (show-FAR)   A trumpet made from a ram's horn, blown during the high Holy Days.

sukkah (sukkot, pl.) (soo-KAH)   A hut or little house built to celebrate Sukkot.

Torah (toe-RAH)   The Five Books of Moses which tell the story of the Jewish people and their laws; also, all teachings. Christians call this the Old Testament.

yarmulkes (YAH-mah-kahs)   Yiddish for the head coverings worn during prayer. Some people wear them all the time. In Hebrew, kippah (singular).

zayde (ZAY-deh)   Grandfather in Yiddish.

zemirot (z'mee-ROTE)   Songs that are traditionally sung during the Friday night Shabbat dinner.